PRESENTS

THE DEFINITIVE GUIDE TO ROBLOX 2026

A TOTALLY INDEPENDENT PUBLICATION

WRITTEN BY NAOMI BERRY | DESIGNED BY JODIE CLARK

A Pillar Box Red Publication

Pillar Box Red Publishing Ltd., 25 Herbert Place, Dublin, D02 AY86. info@pillarboxredpublishing.co.uk

ISBN 978-1-917522-15-1

CONTENTS

GLOSSARY 6-9
AVATARS 10
DESIGN YOUR OWN AVATAR 11

ALL STARS SPOTLIGHT

ALL STARS: ADOPT ME! 12-15
- RARE PET SEARCH 16
- GUESS THE PET 17

ALL STARS: GROW A GARDEN 18-19
- SPRING GARDENING 20
- GARDEN MAZE 21

ALL STARS: TOWER OF HELL 22-23
- MAZE OF HELL 24
- SPOT THE DIFFERENCE 25

ALL STARS: DRESS TO IMPRESS 26-27
- CLOSET CLEAN UP 28
- WHAT'S THE THEME? 29

ALL STARS: PET SIMULATOR 99 30-33
- EGG HATCH MATCH 34
- DREAM PET 35

HONOURABLE MENTIONS I 36-37

ALL STARS: RAINBOW FRIENDS 38-39
- SPOOKY SPOT SCRAMBLE 40
- MONSTER MAKER 41

ALL STARS: DOORS 42-43

ALL STARS: BED WARS 44-45
- ENTITY ESCAPE 46
- BEDWARS BLOCK SEARCH 47

ALL STARS: NATURAL DISASTER SURVIVAL 48-51
- DISASTER CROSSWORD 52
- SPOT THE DISASTER DIFFERENCE 53

HONOURABLE MENTIONS II 54-57
INSIDE THE STUDIO 58-59
DID YOU KNOW? 60-61
PUZZLE ANSWERS 62-63

WELCOME

Welcome, Robloxians! Welcome to the world of Roblox, where your imagination runs the show (Wi-Fi dependent, of course).

Roblox isn't just a game, it's a whole universe; a platform full of whatever game you feel like playing at any moment. Feel like testing your survival skills against a series of natural disasters? Go for it. Want to adopt a tiny pixel baby and raise it as your own? Absolutely. Prefer the thrills of a humdrum pizza shift? Weird flex, but you do you. Or maybe you're in the mood to sprint away from a bunch of murderous colour monsters trying to kidnap you on your school trip. We've all been there, friend.

With over 40 million games (yes, million), it's easy to feel overwhelmed by the sheer scale of it all. That's where this guide steps in. We're spotlighting some of the platform's biggest hits - our certified All Stars - while also shining a light on hidden gems you might not know yet. We'll break down the lingo, walk you through the basics, and even dip into what it takes to make your own game from scratch.

So let's dive in!

GLOSSARY

Roblox isn't just a game - it's a whole universe, full of strange lingo and its own language that has evolved across the platform's 5+ million experiences.

Whether you're a newbie trying to decode what everyone's saying, or a seasoned player who keeps hearing new terms pop up faster than you can say "oof," this glossary has got your back. Time to level up your Robloxian vocabulary!

1V1
Challenge another player to a one-on-one showdown. May the best Robloxian win!

A/D
"Accept or decline" - the classic trading phrase. You might also see A/C (accept or counter) when people are wheeling and dealing.

ADMIN
Short for administrator - these are the powerful players who can moderate servers and sometimes have special commands. Don't mess with them!

AFK
"Away from keyboard" - drop this when you need to step away, or when you're calling out that suspiciously still player who's been standing in the corner for 10 minutes.

ALT
An alternate account separate from your main one. Some people call these burner accounts or sock puppets.

AVATAR
Your digital self in Roblox! The cooler your avatar, the cooler you are (that's definitely how it works, right?).

BEANED
Roblox slang for getting banned. As in, "I got beaned for three days."

BLOXXED
Old-school Roblox speak for getting KO'd. It comes from the classic R6 death animation, so it's practically Ye Olde Robloxian at this point.

CATALOG
The massive shop where you can browse and buy avatar items. RIP to your Robux balance.

DEVELOPER

The creative geniuses behind your favorite experiences. These are the people making the magic happen.

EXPERIENCE

What we call games on Roblox. Each one is a unique world waiting to be explored.

FFA

"Free for all" - every player for themselves! Chaos mode activated.

GFX

Graphics, usually referring to cool artwork or promotional images for games.

GG

"Good game" - the polite thing to say after a match, win or lose. Good sportsmanship never goes out of style.

HR

"High rank" - someone who's climbed the ladder in group hierarchies.

IC

"In character" - when you're staying true to your roleplay persona.

LAG

That annoying delay that makes your avatar move like they're stuck in molasses (or your favourite excuse when you miss the timing for that Tower of Hell jump again).

LIMITED ITEM

The holy grail of Roblox items. These were sold in limited quantities and can't be bought from the catalog anymore. Super valuable and always in demand.

LIMITED (U)

Even rarer than Limited Items. These "Limited Unique" items were designed to be exclusive from day one.

LIMITED U

LMAD

"Let's make a deal" - the opening line for any good trade negotiation.

LUA

The coding language that powers Roblox. It's actually pretty beginner-friendly if you want to try making your own experiences.

MK

Robloxian for "okay." Don't hear it? Say it out loud; you'll get it.

MLG

"Major League Gaming" - used for epic pro plays, though these days it's mostly thrown around sarcastically when someone fails spectacularly.

MODERATOR

Also known as "mods". The people who keep Roblox safe and fun for everyone. They're like digital hall monitors, but cooler.

Check out pages 58-59 for more info on coding with Lua in Roblox Studio!

MR
"Medium rank" - the middle management of group hierarchies.

NFT
In Roblox, this means "not for trade." Don't get it confused with those other NFTs!

NGF
"Not going first" in trades. Everyone wants to avoid getting scammed.

NOOB
A new player, though sometimes used as a general insult. We've all been noobs once!

OBBY
Short for obstacle course - basically platforming heaven. If you haven't rage-quit an obby, are you even a real Robloxian?

OOC
"Out of character" - when you break from roleplay to talk normally.

OOG
"Out of game" - either outside your current experience or outside Roblox entirely.

OOF
The legendary Roblox death sound that became a meme. Also used when something goes wrong. Le oof is the fancy French version, for when you're feeling a touch European in your failure.

PLOX
Roblox slang for "please," usually used ironically or when you're really desperate.

PS
"Private server" - your own personal playground where you control who gets to join.

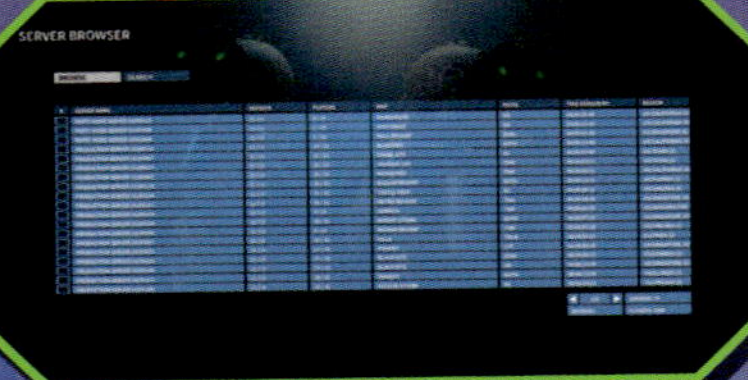

RDM
"Random Death Match" - when someone starts attacking players for no reason. Not cool in most games.

ROBUX
The precious currency that makes the Roblox world go round. Often misspelled as "Bobux" or "Roux", because sometimes you just have to commit to your mistakes.

ROBLOXIAN
That's you! Anyone who plays Roblox games.

RPG
"Roleplay game" - where you become a character and live their story, whether it's pre-written or you make it up as you go.

SFL
"Single file line" - usually barked as a command in military roleplay games.

SPAWN
Where you appear when you join a game or respawn after dying.

STS
"Shoulder to shoulder" - another formation command for organizing players.

TDM
"Team Deathmatch" - organized chaos where teams battle it out.

TERMED
Slang for "terminated" - when someone gets permanently banned. The ultimate punishment.

THUMBNAIL
The image that represents an experience in the games list. First impressions matter!

TT
"Till tomorrow" - a casual way to say goodbye when you're logging off.

UGC
"User Generated Content" - items created by the community rather than Roblox staff.

USD'ER
Someone who spends real money on Limited Items. The high rollers of the trading world.

WIP
"Work in progress" - for when something's not quite finished yet.

WO
Short for "wipeout" - when you get completely demolished.

AVATARS

HOLD UP - before you dive into any games, you've got one big choice to make: your look. In the world of Roblox, your avatar isn't just a character; it's your whole vibe. And with so many styles to choose from, it's almost a game in itself. But how much do you really know about where these iconic avatars came from?

THE R6

Named after its six joints, the R6 was blocky, stiff, and definitely not winning any awards for realism (but hey, it was 2006). Still, it got the job done. Players could pick skin tones, slap on a shirt, and over time, the catalog grew to include faces, hats, and pants. Not the smoothest mover, but a total icon in its own right.

THE R15

Next up was the R15, named with classic Roblox logic for its 15 joints. It dropped in 2016, giving the R6 a legendary ten-year reign before passing the torch. With the R15 came smoother moves, way more animation options, and some pretty slick body-scaling tools that let players tweak proportions and flex their style even more.

THE RTHRO

How do you even begin to explain the Rthro? For starters, it ditched the whole R-plus-joint-count naming thing because, honestly, it's in a league of its own. Rthro stands for Roblox + anthropomorphic, which basically means it's a sleek little digital human. It launched in 2018 and delivered the most realistic design yet, plus tons of customization with Rthro packages and layered 3D clothing.

But even with a glow-up that powerful, the Rthro didn't totally steal the spotlight. A lot of players still ride for the classic avatars, especially since older games and maps weren't really built to handle something as detailed as Rthro. Sometimes, blocky just hits.

DESIGN YOUR OWN AVATAR

The Avatar Shop is packed with endless ways to deck out your Roblox look, but items drop in and out of stock, go Limited (or worse, Limited (U)) and generally serve as a top-tier threat to your Robux wallet. Building your perfect fit can feel more like chasing a moving target, so here's your chance to dream big.

Use the avatar models below to design your ultimate look: no price tags, no limits.

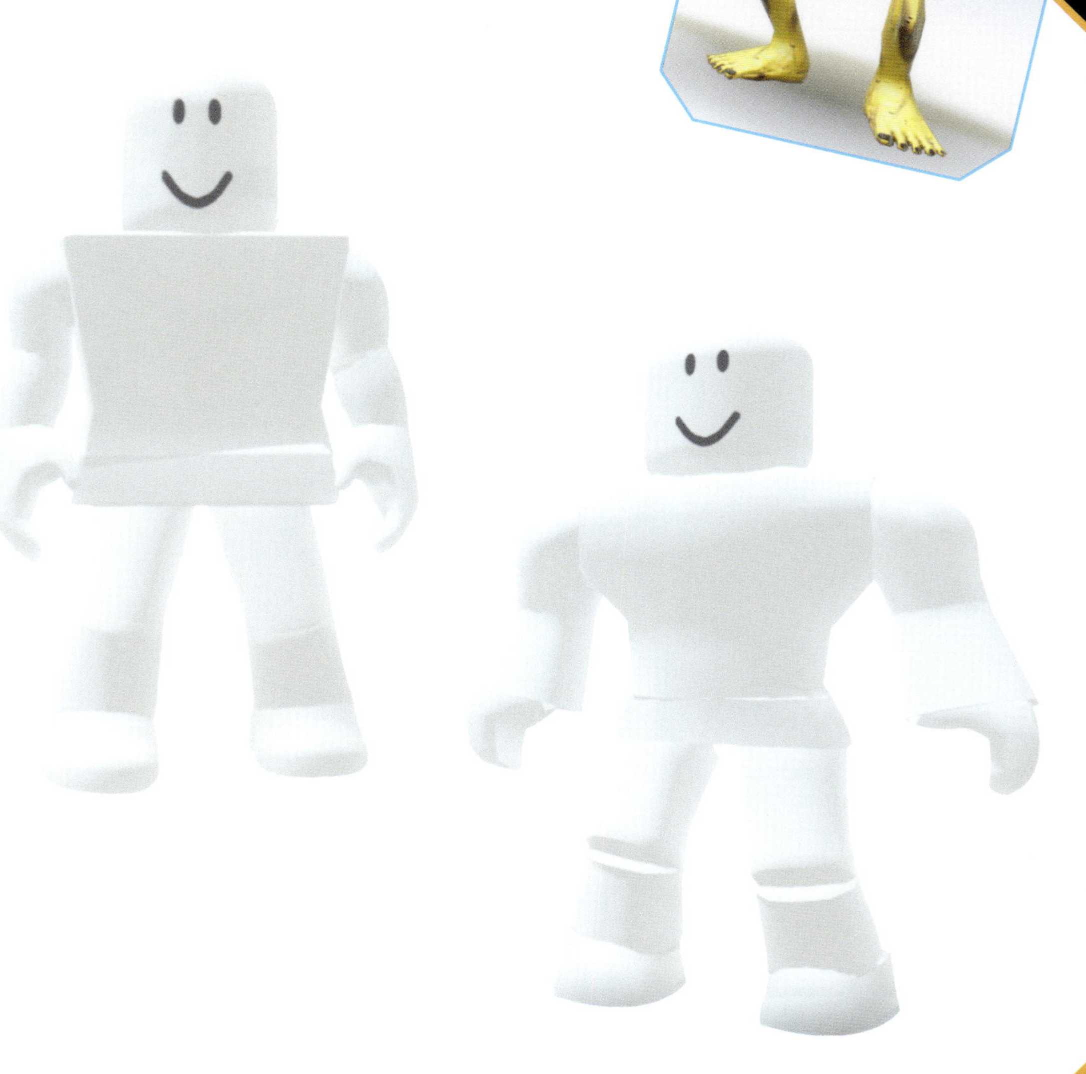

All Stars: Adopt Me!

Is there even any point in introducing this game? Adopt Me! may be all about adopting cute little critters, but the game itself is an absolute beast - becoming one of the most played and recognised titles on the Roblox platform since it first dropped in 2017.

I mean, the game's visit count has surpassed the entire human population several times over now (kind of alarming, actually).

ALL STARS PROFILE

NAME: Adopt Me!
PUBLISHER: Uplift Games
GENRE: RPG
CREATED: July 14th, 2017
VISITS: 39.7 billion +

So, what's so addictive?

Well, it's not just about the title (good games never are) - yes, you can adopt a cutie and raise them, but players can also create and decorate their very own home, enter trade wars with other players and play mini-games and fun activities.

DID YOU KNOW?

Did you know that Adopt Me! was nominated for Favourite Video Game at the 2023 Kids' Choice Awards?

EGGS

How do you like your eggs in the morning? Cracked? Royal? Retired? Ah, you know what kind of eggs we're talking about, right?

All pets in Adopt Me! start out as eggs. Players can get the Starter Egg (their very first egg) from Sir Woofington. From then on, you'll have to cough up some bucks if you want to expand your pet gang

Different egg types contain different types of pets with different types of rarities. There are five permanent egg types in this game:

EGG TYPE	COST (BUCKS)	RARITY	PET RARITY CHANCES
STARTER EGG	FREE	COMMON	Common 100% · Uncommon 0% · Rare 0% · Ultra-rare 0% · Legendary 0%
CRACKED EGG	350	COMMON	Common 45% · Uncommon 33% · Rare 14.5% · Ultra-rare 6% · Legendary .5%
PET EGG	600	RARE	Common 20% · Uncommon 35% · Rare 27% · Ultra-rare 15% · Legendary 3%
RETIRED EGG	600 (VIP ONLY)	RARE	Common 20% · Uncommon 35% · Rare 27% · Ultra-rare 15% · Legendary 3%
ROYAL EGG	1450	LEGENDARY	Common 0% · Uncommon 25% · Rare 37% · Ultra-rare 30% · Legendary 8%

You'll find Cracked Eggs, Pet Eggs, and Royal Eggs in the Pets section of the Nursery, ready for you to trade some Bucks for. But the Retired Egg? That one's got VIP vibes - it only hangs out in the exclusive Nursery VIP Room.

Since Adopt Me! is always cooking up new stuff, you'll also see loads of Limited and Themed eggs show up from time to time (Moon Eggs, Ocean Eggs, Japan Eggs and more). If you're trying to get your hands on a Limited/Theme egg, you can snag one for 750 bucks from the Nursery's Gumball Machine. Oh, and keep an eye out for Event Eggs! These are only available during event periods, and sometimes they're even gifted to the player for free.

PETS

There are so many pets in Adopt Me! it's basically impossible to count them all. But don't worry, there's an easy way to make sense of the madness: the pet rarity system.

COMMON → UNCOMMON → RARE → ULTRA-RARE → LEGENDARY

This same scale also applies to other in-game items. Usually, the rarer the pet, the more valuable it is (if you're into trading and flexing). But honestly, who's judging if your favorite pet is just a googly-eyed rock? Love doesn't follow a rarity chart.

You'll find out your pet's rarity the moment it hatches. And while it's all based on luck, pricier eggs do tend to have better odds of giving you something rare.

MAKING BUCKS

If you're planning to raise a whole crew of baby pets, good news - you'll be stacking bucks along the way! There are tons of ways to earn money in Adopt Me!, but here are some of the easiest (and actually worth it) methods to boost your wallet:

PLAY AS A BABY

Want to double your cash? Switch your role to a baby. You'll earn twice the bucks for every task you complete, which means more coins and cuteness all at once.

BLUE TASKS

These are your money-makers. Blue tasks don't just help your pet grow, they also pay out 6 to 7 bucks each. There are four types: Hungry, Thirsty, Sleepy, and Dirty. Your home's already got a crib and shower for Sleepy and Dirty tasks, and as for food and drinks? Either hit the store or stock up your house with handy appliances. Easy peasy.

ORANGE TASKS

These are the high-rollers of Adopt Me! tasks. They're location-based (like Camping, Hot Spring, School, Sick, Pizza Party, Salon, and Bored) and they dish out 12 to 18 bucks each. Prioritize these whenever they pop up, especially Camping - it has the highest payout and counts toward Sleepy if you bring a pet along. Win-win.

MONEY TREES

A Money Tree might seem pricey at 1,450 bucks, but it's a long-term money maker. It gives you 8 bucks every in-game day (that's about every ten minutes), up to 100 bucks in a real day. If you're planning to stick around in the game, it basically pays for itself and then some. Future You will thank you for this one.

PERSONAL TASKS

Check your personal task board for these. They vary a lot in what they ask and how much they pay, but some can give you a solid boost if you knock them out between regular tasks.

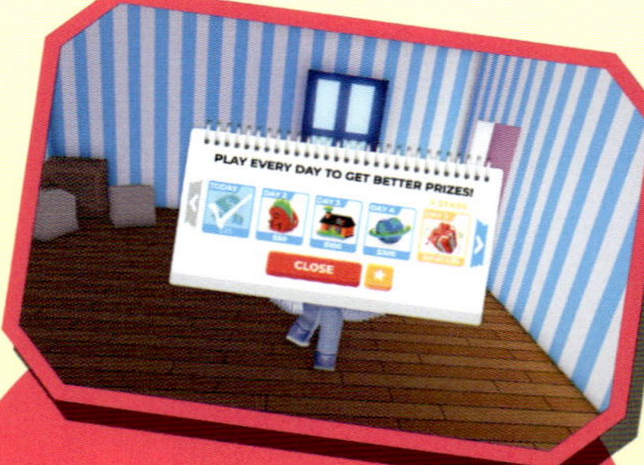

LOGIN REWARDS

Get paid for showing up. Sweet. The longer your daily login streak, the bigger the rewards. Easy money for zero effort? Yes, please.

NEWBORNS AND NEONS

When a pet hatches, it starts off as a tiny Newborn, but it won't stay that cute lil' baby forever. Every pet in Adopt Me! grows through different life stages, and while some of them sound pretty normal... things definitely get weird real fast. Here's the full glow-up timeline (and it'll be pretty clear when it goes from pretty normal to weird real fast):

POST-TEEN → FULL-GROWN → NEON → MEGA NEON

Pets grow from squishy little Newborns to full-grown legends just by playing the game and knocking out tasks. The catch? The rarer your pet, the more work it takes to level them up, to get ready to hustle if you're trying to grow your very own Mega Neon squad.

NEWBORN TO FULL-GROWN

PET RARITY	AMOUNT OF TASKS
COMMON	56
UNCOMMON	70
RARE	150
ULTRA-RARE	178
LEGENDARY	189

Once your pet hits full-grown, the real magic begins - quite literally. To get a Neon or Mega Neon pet, you've got to do a little crafting. Head over to the Neon Cave (you'll find it tucked under the big bridge on Adoption Island), and there, you can combine four full-grown pets of the same species to create one shiny Neon pet. Want to go even neon-er? Combine four of the same Neon pets to unlock a Mega Neon masterpiece.

ADOPT ME!
RARE PET SEARCH

There are tons of pets waiting to be adopted in Adopt Me!, but only a few reach legendary status. Think you've got an eagle eye? Try spotting some of the rarer pets hidden in the wordsearch below!

Need a little help? Flip to pages 62–63 for all the answers.

Y	A	N	K	Y	L	O	S	A	U	R	U	S	D
K	A	P	P	A	K	I	D	U	E	C	O	K	I
D	K	O	A	V	P	A	R	A	K	E	E	T	O
D	R	C	N	E	G	L	E	E	E	L	S	U	O
F	L	E	B	A	H	I	V	A	D	E	N	O	U
E	Y	L	I	G	R	I	B	O	P	P	Y	K	E
E	N	O	O	N	L	W	P	B	J	H	A	C	S
S	X	T	A	R	D	O	H	L	O	A	J	E	R
H	Z	E	O	S	E	E	H	A	Y	N	E	G	O
U	L	C	E	Z	B	S	E	V	L	T	U	A	H
S	K	S	W	A	N	E	K	R	L	D	L	Y	R
K	K	N	U	M	P	I	H	C	K	E	B	B	E
Y	E	R	P	R	T	A	R	S	I	E	R	S	M
N	B	A	S	I	L	I	S	K	Y	Y	N	Z	A

ANKYLOSAURUS
BASILISK
BLUE JAY
CHIPMUNK
ELEPHANT
EVIL ROCK
FEESH

GECKO
GIBBON
HUSKY
KAPPAKID
LYNX
MERHORSE
NARWHAL

OCELOT
PARAKEET
REINDEER
SWAN
TARSIER
ZEOPOD

GUESS THE PET

Can you guess the Adopt Me! Pet from the clues below?
Check out pages 62-63 for answers.

1 I'm small, white, and I follow you around saying "quack"!

WHO AM I?

....

5 I have a magical horn and sparkly hooves. I'm a favourite of fairy lovers!

WHO AM I?

....

2 I breathe fire and love to fly. I'm a legendary pet from a fantasy world!

WHO AM I?

....

6 I wear a tuxedo, waddle on land, and love chilly weather.

WHO AM I?

....

3 I'm a fluffy magical fox with nine tails and I'm super rare!

WHO AM I?

....

7 I'm a multi-coloured bird that was once found in the Jungle Zone.

WHO AM I?

....

4 I'm a big blue beast with horns and I love to stomp around.

WHO AM I?

....

8 I'm orange with stripes and a big roar, but I'm still cuddly in your backpack!

WHO AM I?

....

ALL STARS: GROW A GARDEN

It hasn't been long since Grow a Garden first dropped on the platform, but it's already skyrocketed to becoming one of Roblox's most popular experiences. Whether you're into colourful blooms, buzzing bees, or cute critters, this game is all about watching your garden come alive and grow into something amazing.

At its core, Grow a Garden is a relaxing and rewarding game where you plant seeds, water your plants, and watch them sprout into beautiful flowers and vegetables. But it's much more than just gardening - players can decorate their space with fun items, explore different biomes, and even collect special garden pets that bring your garden to life.

ALL STARS PROFILE

NAME: Grow a Garden!

PUBLISHER: The Garden Game

GENRE: Simulation

CREATED: March 26th, 2025

VISITS: 7.6 billion +

DID YOU KNOW?

Grow a Garden was developed by a sixteen year old?! If that inspires you to try making your own game, check out our chapter on Roblox Studio on pages 58-59.

PLANTING YOUR FIRST GARDEN

1. **CHOOSE YOUR SEEDS:** At the start, you get a handful of seeds to plant. Each seed grows into a different type of plant, so mix and match to see what looks best!
2. **WATER YOUR PLANTS:** Keep your garden hydrated by watering daily. Plants need water to grow big and strong.
3. **HARVEST AND COLLECT:** When your plants bloom or bear fruit, harvest them to earn in-game currency. You can use this to buy new seeds, decorations, and special items.
4. **DECORATE YOUR GARDEN:** Personalize your space with benches, fences, fountains, and even garden gnomes! The more you decorate, the happier your garden feels.

PRO-GARDENING TIPS

ROTATE YOUR CROPS: Some plants grow faster or better when alternated. Try planting different seeds in nearby spots to keep your garden thriving.

VISIT FRIENDS' GARDENS: Check out other players' gardens for inspiration and trading opportunities. You might spot rare plants or cool design ideas!

LOOK FOR SPECIAL EVENTS: The game often runs seasonal events with unique seeds and items. Keep an eye out for those limited-time opportunities to make your garden one-of-a-kind.

TAKE CARE OF YOUR PETS: Some rare garden pets can help speed up plant growth or find hidden treasures. Make sure to feed and play with them to keep them happy.

GARDEN THEME IDEAS

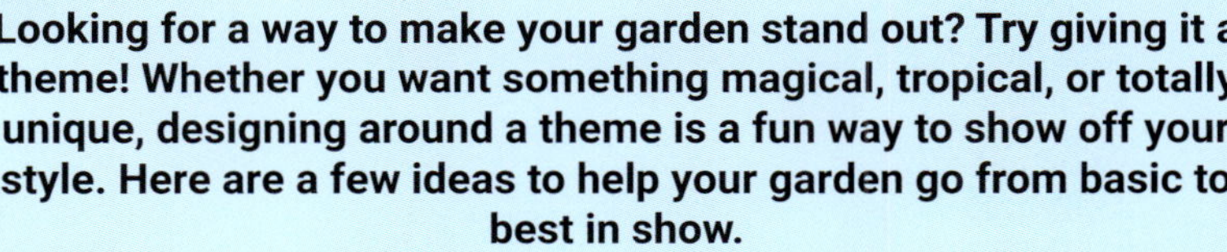

Looking for a way to make your garden stand out? Try giving it a theme! Whether you want something magical, tropical, or totally unique, designing around a theme is a fun way to show off your style. Here are a few ideas to help your garden go from basic to best in show.

FAIRY TALE GARDEN

Fill your garden with glowing mushrooms, twinkling lights, and magical flowers. Add tiny fairy houses and sparkly paths for a whimsical vibe.

TROPICAL PARADISE

Plant bright, exotic flowers and tall palm trees. Use beach chairs, tiki torches, and fountains to create a sunny getaway.

CLASSIC ENGLISH GARDEN

Go for neatly trimmed hedges, rose bushes, and cozy benches. Add vintage lanterns and birdbaths for timeless charm.

MODERN MINIMALIST

Keep it clean and simple with sleek pathways, geometric flower beds, and elegant planters. Use monochrome colors and minimalist decor.

JUNGLE ADVENTURE

Grow wild, leafy plants and vines. Scatter jungle statues and wooden bridges to make it feel like an exploration site.

SPRING GARDENING

It's Springtime and the garden is in full bloom! Can you group all the crops and pets you can see in the garden?

Check out pages 62-63 for answers.

GARDEN MAZE

Can you make your way through the garden maze to reach your pets?

Check out pages 62-63 for solutions!

START HERE

END HERE

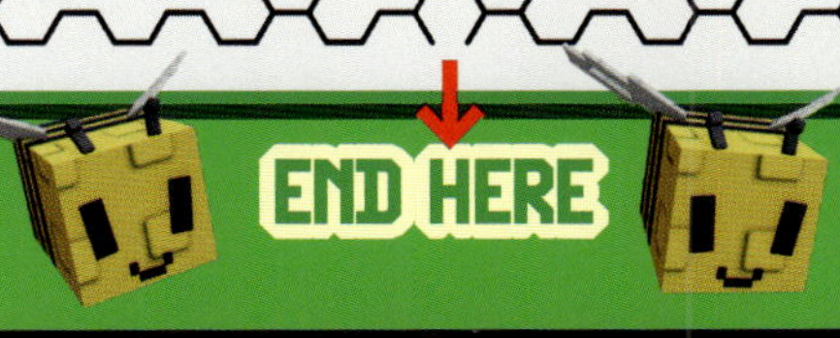

ALL STARS:

TOWER OF HELL

Ready to rage, race, and possibly fall into the void (very likely, to be honest)? Welcome to Tower of Hell, one of Roblox's wildest and most addictive obstacle course games. There are no checkpoints. No second chances. Just you, the tower, and a timer counting down like your life depends on it!

In Tower of Hell, you compete to climb to the top of a tall, ever-changing tower made of tricky jumps, spinning lasers, narrow platforms, and all kinds of evil parkour nightmares.

ALL STARS PROFILE

NAME: Tower of Hell
PUBLISHER: YXCeptional Studios
GENRE: Adventure
CREATED: June 19th, 2018
VISITS: 25.4 billion +

HOW IT'S BUILT TO BREAK YOU

Every tower in Tower of Hell is made from randomly-selected sections, each designed to test a different skill: be it timing, precision or just the strength of your patience and will to live. These different sections snap together like blocks, so no two towers are ever the same.

It's part puzzle, part obstacle course, part "why did I just do that?!" And once you start recognizing the stages, you'll develop your own strategies and shortcuts like a real obby detective.

DID YOU KNOW?

Tower of Hell has secret badge rooms for players who complete the tower under certain conditions.

TOWER OF HELL LINGO

Want to sound like you know what you're talking about? Here's a quick rundown of some of the most commonly used Tower of Hell-specific terms you'll come across in chat:

PRO SKIP
A risky move that skips a whole section (only for the truly brave)

RAGE JUMP
That one dumb jump you know you can make, but keep failing anyway

CAMPER
A player who reaches the top and just stands there to annoy everyone

RUSH ROUND
When someone finishes early and speeds up the timer (cue panic!)

HALO
A glowing ring earned by beating every stage in a category

SWEATY
A player who's way too good and finishes towers in like 40 seconds flat (no one's impressed, Steve)

TOP TOWER TIPS

Want to get good at scaling the tower? These advanced tricks will help you conquer even the nastiest of tower combos.

If you're serious about speed, get comfortable using shift lock or playing in first-person mode. It gives you more control over your jumps and camera angles, especially on narrow platforms or tiny ledges.

Learn how to wrap around poles and walls by jumping at sharp angles and rotating midair (this move shows up in a ton of harder stages).

Start practicing ladder flicks, too. It's a flashy move that lets you launch off ladders without climbing all the way up (great for saving time in race situations).

If you're playing on Pro Towers or in custom servers, look for ways to skip sections with clever jumps. Not every shortcut is obvious, but some can help you leap from the bottom of one section to the top of the next.

And if you're on a public server where someone speeds up the timer, don't panic. Breathe, focus, and don't rush - most mistakes happen when you're chasing the clock.

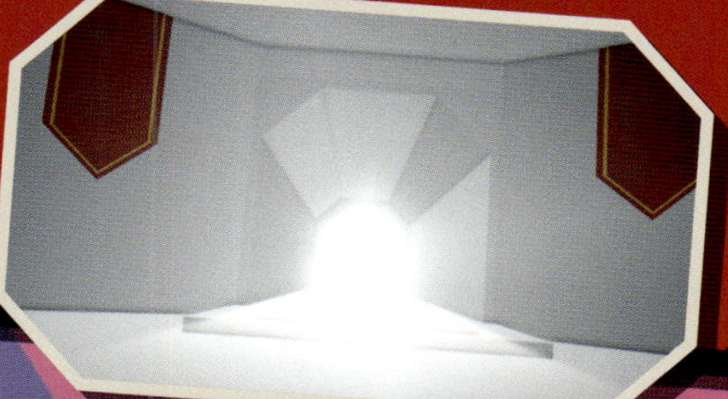

MAZE OF HELL

Can you make it to the top of the tower maze without getting knocked by any obstacles along the way? ***Flip to pages 62–63 to see how it's done.***

SPOT THE DIFFERENCE

Can you find the eight differences between these two shots?
Check out answers on pages 62-63.

ALL STARS: DRESS TO IMPRESS

ALL STARS PROFILE

NAME: Dress to Impress
PUBLISHER: Dress to Impress Group
GENRE: Roleplay & Avatar Sim
CREATED: October 18, 2023
VISITS: 7.2 billion +

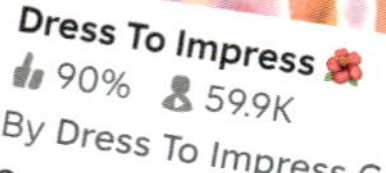

Get ready to strut your stuff, because Dress to Impress is the ultimate Roblox fashion showdown! In this game, you're not just picking clothes - you're creating a lewk.

The game throws you a theme and gives you a few minutes to build the perfect outfit using tons of clothes, accessories, hairstyles, and even pets. Once the clock runs out, you step onto the runway, and the judges (other players!) vote for the best look. It's fashion, fun, and fierce competition all rolled into one.

Whether you're going for glam, sporty, steampunk or regency era (hey, those categories can get really broad), every outfit is your chance to shine.

DID YOU KNOW?

In 2024, Dress to Impress had an official collab with global pop star Charli XCX to promote her summer album (and lifestyle mantra) Brat.

HOW TO SLAY THE RUNWAY

KNOW YOUR THEME

The key to winning? Stick to the theme but make it your style. Put your own spin on the category to serve up something truly chic and unique.

This round's theme is: Urban Legends

MIX AND MATCH

Dress to Impress gives you tons of options, from bright neon jackets to sparkly boots. Try mixing colors and patterns to stand out. Sometimes the wildest combos catch the judges' eyes.

ACCESSORIES, ACCESSORIES, ACCESSORIES

Hats, glasses, pets, wings - accessories can make your outfit pop. Got a flashy parrot or a sparkly tiara? Use it! Just make sure it fits your look.

LAYER UP

Wearing multiple clothing items like jackets over shirts adds style depth. All the best players are creating custom pieces by layering as many different pieces as they can get their hands on.

SERVE FACE

Facial expressions are just as much part of the outfit as your accessories. Picking a confident or happy face can actually help judges like your character more.

PRACTICE MAKES PERFECT

Try different styles in free dress mode to find your fashion vibe. The more outfits you create, the better you get at impressing the crowd.

HOW TO UNLOCK COOL CLOTHES FAST

Win runway contests - each win can unlock new styles.

Complete daily challenges for special rewards.

Level up by playing more rounds to get new item packs.

Check out special holiday events for limited-time gear you can't get anywhere else.

DID YOU KNO

Dress to Impress is relatively new on the scene but it made a big impression. At its first Roblox Innovation Awarc in 2024, it won Builderma Choice of Excellence, Be Creative Direction and Best new Experience.

CLOSET CLEAN UP

The Dress to Impress closet has seen one too many mad rushes to meet themes - it's time to clean up! Can you sort out all the clothes and accessories and tidy up a bit?

Check out pages 62-63 for help.

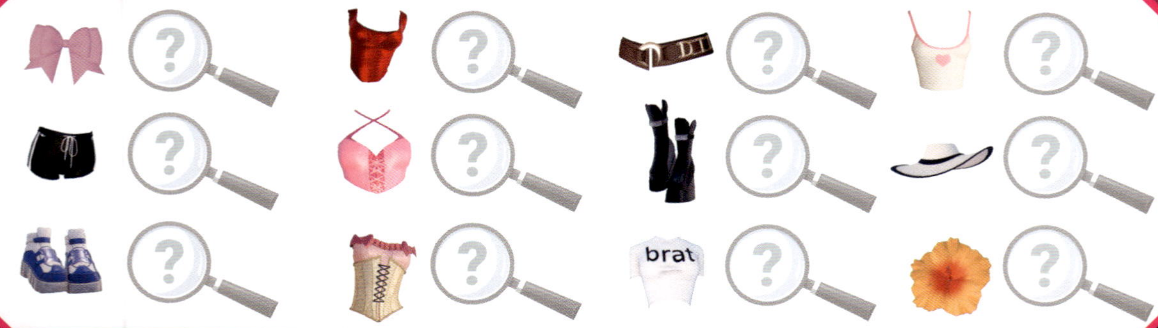

WHAT'S THE THEME?

The key to success in Dress to Impress is to dress for the occasion. Can you identify these themes from the clues below? We've given you the first letter or number of the theme as a hint, too.

When you're done, check out pages 62-63 to see if you truly are the fashionista of our times.

1. Flapper dresses, feathers and pearls. — R _ _ _ _ _ _ _ 2 _ _
2. Experimental and abstract works of art. — A _ _ _ _ - G _ _ _ _
3. Sleek and chic for the classroom. — B _ _ _ T _ S _ _ _ _ _
4. Sassy, rebellious and plenty of attitude. — B _ _ _
5. Soft, vintage and plenty of knitwear. — C _ _ _ _ _ _ _ _ _ _
6. Adorable pastel looks with playful details. — K _ _ _ _ _
7. Scholarly and sophisticated. — D _ _ _ A _ _ _ _ _ _ _
8. Bright, beachy, floral and sunny. — T _ _ _ _ _ _ _
9. Corsets, lace, and we better not see ankle. — V _ _ _ _ _ _ _ _ _
10. Dark, bold, and a little bit evil. — V _ _ _ _ _ _

ALL STARS: PET SIMULATOR 99!

Pet Simulator X (or PSX, if you're in the know) used to rule the Roblox pet world right alongside Adopt Me! It was one of the biggest, most popular experiences on the platform. But things change and times move on, and so did the game. In 2022, BIG Games Pets launched the next chapter: Pet Simulator 99!, a fresh sequel with even more pets, worlds, and surprises to discover.

ALL STARS PROFILE

NAME:	Pet Simulator 99!
PUBLISHER:	BIG Games Pets
GENRE:	Simulation
CREATED:	February 5th, 2022
VISITS:	2.1 billion +

HOW DO YOU LIKE YOUR EGGS?

PS99 starts with having the player choose two starter pets, but any additional pets from there will mean you need to buy and hatch some eggs.

There are a ridiculous amount of different egg types in this game; each world has its own set of eggs, and each egg contains different types of pets and rarities. Your first egg type is the Cracked Egg, but you'll soon find yourself moving on from there pretty quickly, unlocking new eggs that hold rarer and stronger pets (but cost more money to hatch, of course).

DID YOU KNOW?

There are also a bunch of item eggs and event eggs available at different times of the year, so make sure to check the developer notes on the game's launch page to see what's available when you log in.

WORLD EXPLORER

The whole point of gathering your pet squad is to travel through the different biomes of the PS99 world. 2025 brought the game a brand new world in Update 59, but before you ever reach it, you'll have to work your way through the biomes on the way.

SPAWN WORLD:

Ah, home sweet home. This is the first world the player drops in PS99. It also hosts most of the game's events, so you'll have plenty of reasons to come back here. There are 99 areas in this world and 112 eggs.

TECH WORLD:

Tech World is the second world, and has 100 areas and 100 eggs.

VOID WORLD:

This special world is more of a hub than a regular world, with 8 sub-worlds accessible via portal (Prison World, Obby World, Hacker World, Millionaire World, Kawaii World, Elemental World, Olympus World and Doodle World). This was the last world in the game for quite some time, until...

FANTASY WORLD:

The newest world of the game, dropped this year with Update 59.

Don't forget to use your hoverboard! This lets you zoom through areas and worlds fast, collect drops quickly, and waste less time between farming spots.

MONEY MONEY MONEY

COINS AND BARS

At the end of the day, PS99 is all about earning some digital dollars. With so many different currencies in the game, you'll want to know your diamonds from your fantasy coins if you want your pet squad to level up and live their best lives.

Each world starts with a base currency (Coin), which then multiplies into higher values of currency from there (usually Bars).

A quick heads-up: the numbers in this table might very well be some of the wildest numbers you have ever seen in your life. For real. But don't worry, you go from zero to quintillion (!) real quick in this game.

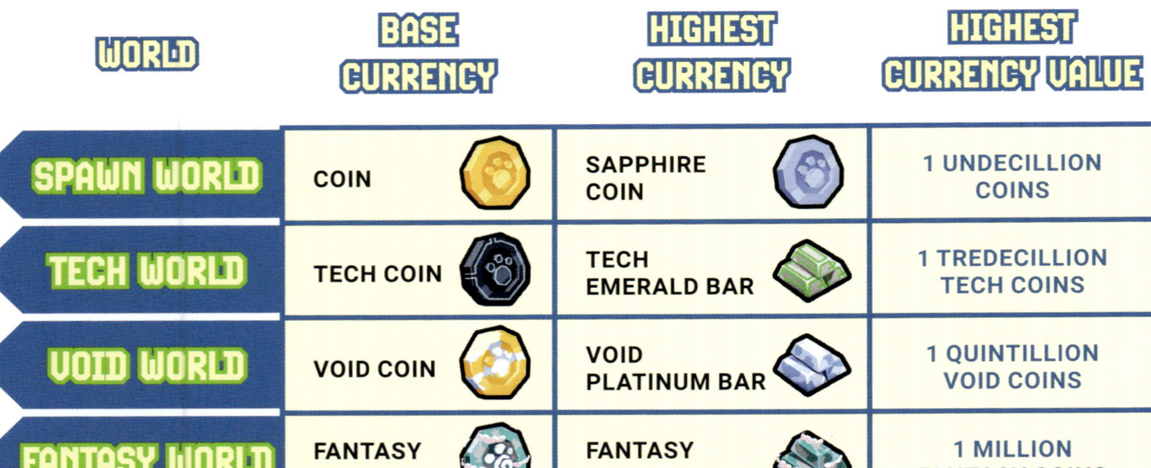

WORLD	BASE CURRENCY	HIGHEST CURRENCY	HIGHEST CURRENCY VALUE
SPAWN WORLD	COIN	SAPPHIRE COIN	1 UNDECILLION COINS
TECH WORLD	TECH COIN	TECH EMERALD BAR	1 TREDECILLION TECH COINS
VOID WORLD	VOID COIN	VOID PLATINUM BAR	1 QUINTILLION VOID COINS
FANTASY WORLD	FANTASY COIN	FANTASY BAR	1 MILLION FANTASY COINS

DIAMONDS

  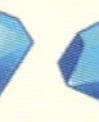     

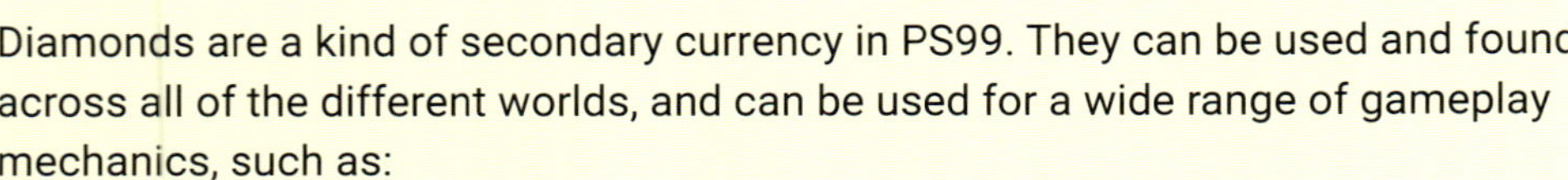

Diamonds are a kind of secondary currency in PS99. They can be used and found across all of the different worlds, and can be used for a wide range of gameplay mechanics, such as:

-  **Buying Diamond Eggs**
-  **Buying upgrades**
-  **Levelling up enchants and potions**
- **Expanding pet equips**
-  **Trading with players**

DID YOU KNOW?

The maximum number of Diamonds a player can hold at one time is 1,000,000,000,000 (that's one trillion, if you're curious).

Keep an eye out for Shiny Relics hidden all over each world! Collecting 5 will boost your chances of hatching a rare shiny pet. And the best part? The boost is permanent and stackable. With over 150 relics out there, it definitely pays to explore every corner!

MINI-GAMES

Pet Simulator 99 mixes things up by throwing in mini-games as you travel through different areas. These fun little sidequests take inspiration from some of Roblox's most popular game genres, so there's always something fresh to try.

Complete a mini-game and you'll earn rewards like special items, gifts, and sometimes even rare pets! Each world comes with its own unique set of mini-games, so keep exploring and don't skip the fun.

WORLD	MINI-GAMES
SPAWN WORLD	Classic Obby, Minefield, Jungle Obby, Atlantis, Fishing, Digsite, Pyramid Obby, Icy Obby, Sled Race, Chest Rush, Stairway to Heaven, Cart Ride, Advanced Digsite, Lucky Blocks!, Advanced Fishing
TECH WORLD	Hoverboard Obby, Diamond Wheel, Chest Raid, Claw Machine, Treasure Hideout, Enchant Empowering, Hacker Obby
VOID WORLD	Bank Heist, Tiki Egg Hunt, Jungle Boss Fight, Millionaire Race, Tokyo Alley, Woodcutting, Doodle Battle

All the mini-games have a cooldown or a set start time, so if the one you're after isn't ready yet, just swing back later and give it another shot!

PRO-TIP!

Don't sleep on the auto features. Auto Hatch, Auto Tap, and Auto Fuse save you tons of time (and finger cramps). If you've got the game passes or earn them during events, use them!

EGG HATCH MATCH

It's hatching season! Can you match the pets to the eggs they hatched from?

Answers can be found on pages 62-63!

DREAM PET

There are always fresh eggs and new pets hatching their way into Pet Simulator 99, so why not dream up your own? Create your very own egg type and design a custom pet to go with it. Will it be cute, chaotic, or just plain weird? Your egg, your rules!

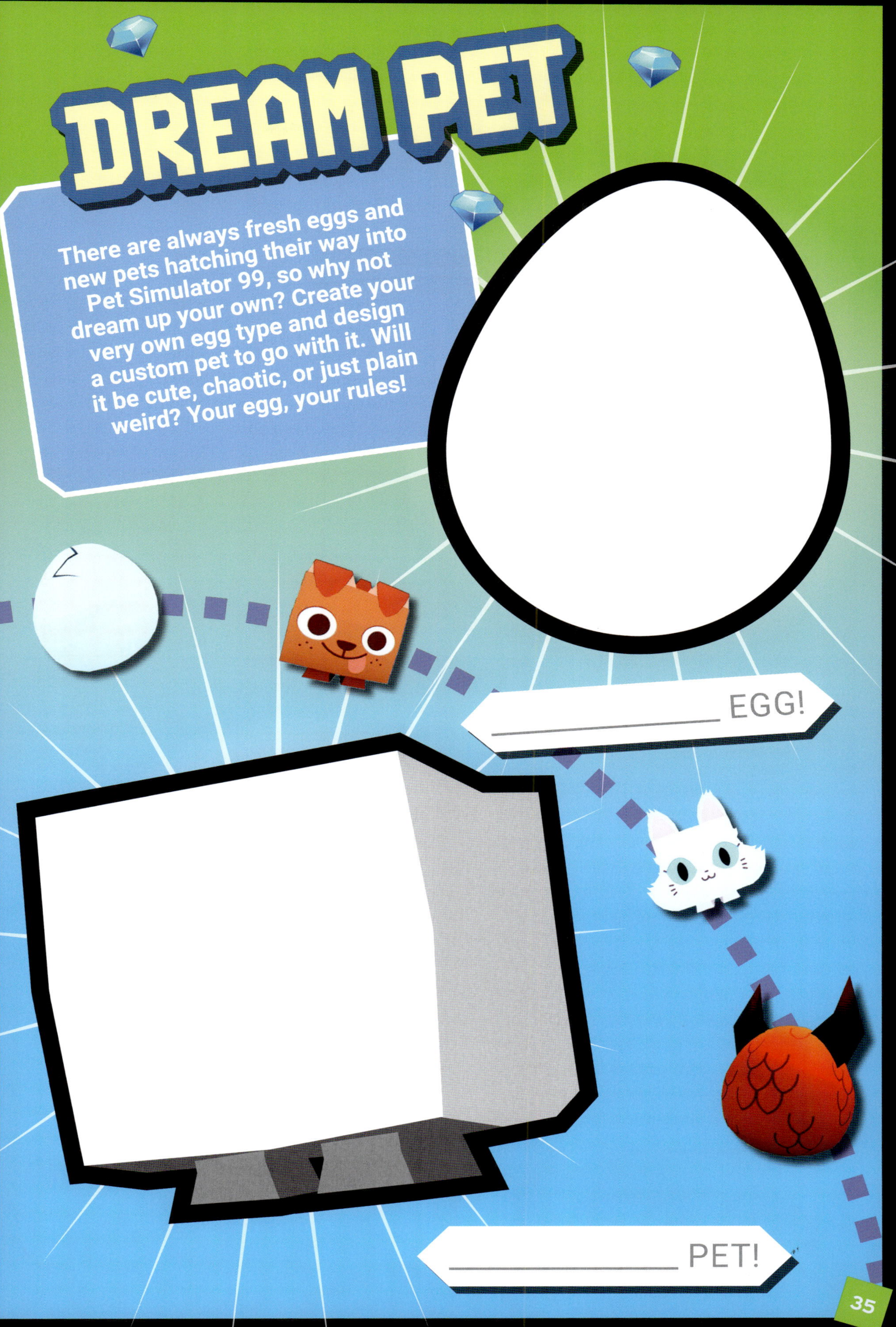

HONOURABLE MENTIONS I

Sure, we've put the spotlight on our All Stars - those massive, chart-topping experiences that everyone's talking about. But here's the thing: they're literally just a tiny speck in the enormous universe that is Roblox.

Those big names? Total certified bangers, no doubt. But sometimes the real gems are hiding in the shadows - the lesser-known, under-the-radar experiences that might just scratch that gaming itch in ways you never expected. Think of it like discovering an amazing indie band before they blow up, except with more explosions and probably more oofs.

PHANTOM FORCES

PUBLISHER:
StyLiS Studios

GENRE: FPS

If you're craving some serious FPS action, Phantom Forces is about to become your new obsession. This isn't some knock-off shooter - we're talking Battlefield 4-level intensity packed into a Roblox experience. You'll pick your side in the eternal war between the Phantoms and the Ghosts, then dive headfirst into chaos across six different game modes. Whether you're grinding Team Deathmatch, dominating in Flare Domination, or clutching it out in Kill Confirmed, there's always a new way to prove you're the ultimate soldier. Plus, those seasonal modes keep things fresh when you need a break from the regular mayhem. Fair warning: once you start, good luck putting it down.

THEME PARK TYCOON 2

PUBLISHER:
Den_S

GENRE: Building

Ever daydreamed about running your own theme park? Well, stop dreaming and start building! This building legend lets you craft everything from death-defying roller coaster peaks to the tiniest decorative bushes lining your queue paths (these details matter; you don't have to convince me). But here's the catch - you can't just build the coolest park ever and call it a day. You've got to think like a business genius too, because even the most mind-blowing attractions won't matter if you're bleeding money faster than guests are screaming on your rides. It's the perfect blend of creative chaos and cold, hard capitalism.

BLOX FRUITS

PUBLISHER:
Gamer Robot Inc

GENRE:
Adventure

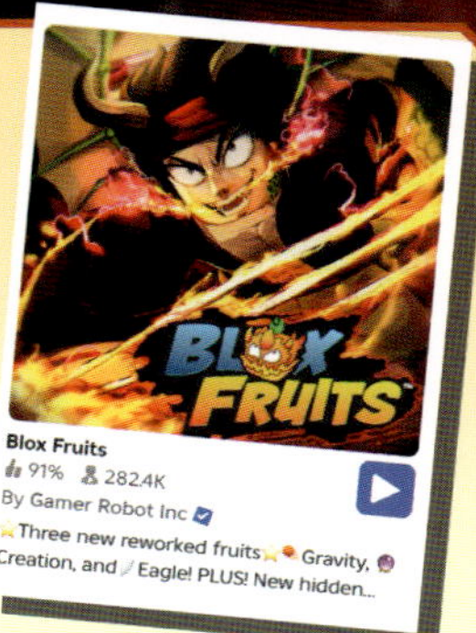

Blox Fruits exploded onto the scene back on 2019, and has since skyrocketed to become one of Roblox's most addictive phenomenons. And honestly? We totally saw it coming. I mean, who wouldn't want to live out their One Piece fantasies, sailing the high seas in search of legendary devil fruits while grinding to become the most legendary pirate (or marine, no bias here) to ever exist? It's like someone took everything awesome about anime adventures and cranked it up to eleven. No wonder millions of players are completely hooked on leveling up their powers and conquering the ocean.

WORK AT A PIZZA PLACE

PUBLISHER:
Dued1

GENRE:
Town & City

WAAPP (because who has time for all those syllables?) is the definition of a Roblox OG - this legend has been serving up virtual pizza since 2008! Don't let the simple concept fool you though. Sure, you're just making pizzas, taking orders, and decorating your apartment with your hard-earned cash, but there's something weirdly addictive about the whole thing. Maybe you'll start as a cashier, work your way up to manager, then say "forget it" and become a delivery driver instead. And here's a pro tip: there are secret spots hidden around the residential area that most players never find. It's like a pizza-scented treasure hunt!

ALL STARS: RAINBOW FRIENDS

Welcome to Rainbow Friends, where the brightest, happiest colours are hiding something seriously sinister. What starts as a field trip to Odd World quickly turns into a wild escape mission when you're trapped inside a strange factory full of creepy rainbow-coloured monsters. Your goal? Solve puzzles, avoid the Rainbow Friends, and make it out alive.

Each round of the game takes you deeper into the factory. You'll need to collect missing items, unlock doors, and stay out of sight - oh, and all while being hunted (of course). But don't worry, you're not alone! You'll be playing with other Roblox fans who are also trying to survive. Team up, split up, and think fast; every second counts.

ALL STARS PROFILE

NAME: Rainbow Friends
PUBLISHER: Roy & Charcle
GENRE: Adventure
CREATED: November 14, 2021
VISITS: 4.2 billion +

PRO-TIP!

Players often drop items when they get caught, so keep your eyes open!

DID YOU KNOW?

Hey, did you know there's a secret test place in the map where you can find two unused monsters? There's "Pink", an alien-like monster, and a weird human sized duck. Chapter 3 monsters, perhaps?

MEET THE RAINBOW FRIENDS

You'll meet some weird and wild monsters on your escape mission, and each one acts differently. Learning how each moves is key to staying safe!

BLUE

This guy is usually the first monster players run into. He's big, he's slow, he drools everywhere (an absolute delight), and he's always chasing.

GREEN

He may be blind, but he can still get his long-armed hands on you, especially if you make noise.

ORANGE

This guy is fast and loves to zoom up on you out of nowhere. You'll know when he's on the loose thanks to his trail. Keep him fed to keep him off your tail.

PURPLE

This vent-lurker grabs innocent players who wander too close.

YELLOW

With a propeller on his back, Yellow will grab any player he catches and fly them to his nest for a little snack (on you, not for you, FYI).

CYAN

Though she has no arms, she's still able to chase you down.

RED

Master Monster, Red stays behind the scenes, but he's watching everything and pulling all the strings.

HOW TO STAY ALIVE

The best way to win is to stay alert. Turn up your volume and listen out for footsteps, roars, or weird sounds - they're a surefire sign that a Rainbow Friend is nearby. If you hear Orange's alarm or see Purple's vent hands, hide fast!

The factory is filled with hiding spots, but you'll need to be quick. Lockers and boxes can save you, but timing is everything. The more rounds you play, the more you'll start to learn the best hiding spots, secret shortcuts, and puzzle tricks.

And survival is a lot easier when you play together. Try to cooperate and plan with the other players to tackle the night's goals. You know what they say: team work makes the dream work.

SPOOKY SPOT SCRAMBLE

Can you unscramble the names of these spooky spots from Rainbow Friends? We'll give you the first letter as a hint!

You can find the answers on pages 62-63.

1. HCEMLOK WDOOS
2. B'SULE CLESAT
3. MUMSUE
4. TEHEATR
5. ODD WDRLO
6. PSUP'LRE LRAI
7. OAS'RNEG CVNARE CRSTAOE
8. GRNSE'E DPOR TWREO

MONSTER MAKER

Rainbow Friends has had some iconic mascot monsters... but can you design a new one to join the rainbow critter crew?

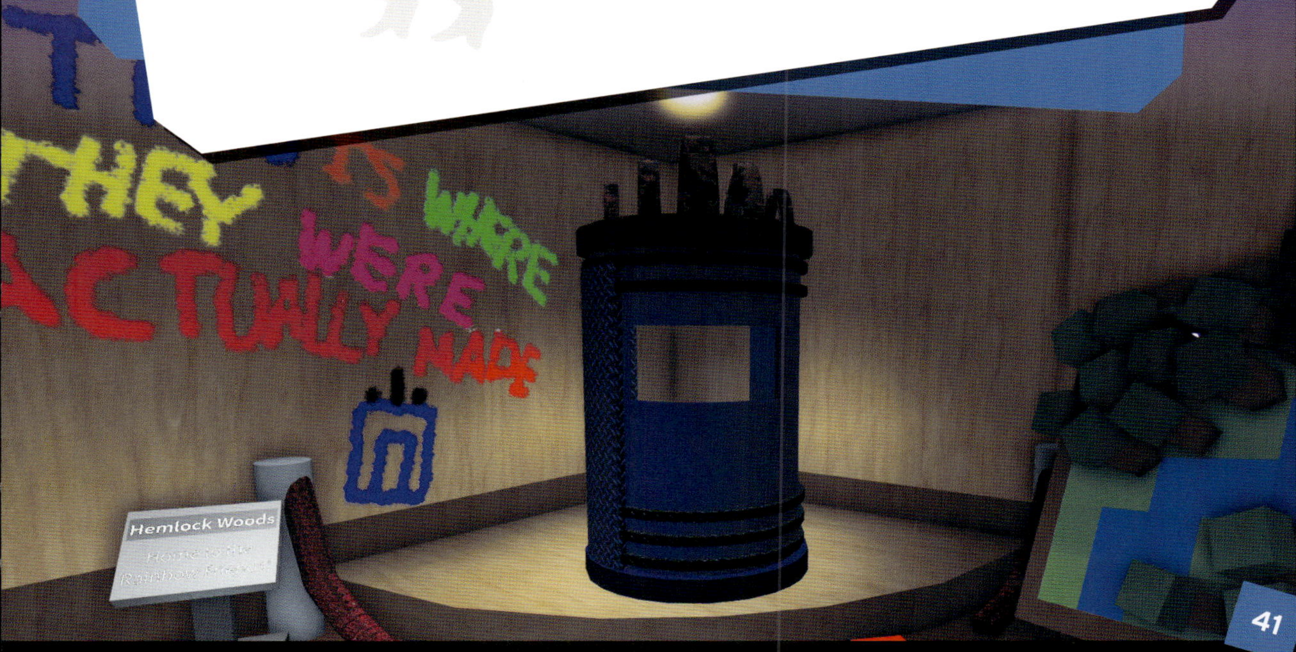

ALL STARS: DOORS

DOORS is one of Roblox's most thrilling horror games. I know what you're probably thinking: thrilling? Opening doors? Trust us; it's so much more than that.

This atmospheric adventure drops you into a haunted hotel with one simple goal: reach Door 100. The catch? Well, who knows what's lurking behind each of them? Each door could very well be your last. Are you brave enough to open the next?

ALL STARS PROFILE

NAME:	DOORS
PUBLISHER:	LSPLASH
GENRE:	Survival
CREATED:	March 14th, 2021
VISITS:	6.5 billion +

THE HOTEL

KNOCK IF YOU DARE...

You start in an elevator with up to three other players. Once the game begins, you'll explore a series of randomly generated rooms by (you guessed it) opening doors. But take your time! Some rooms you'll find to be very safe. Others... not so much.

The hotel layout is randomly generated each time you play, so memorizing rooms won't help; no two DOORS runs are ever the same.

KNOW YOUR ENTITIES

Any horror is only as scary as its monsters, and the ones in DOORS (better known as "entities") are right up there with some of the spookiest specters in gaming. Each entity behaves differently, and learning their patterns is key to survival.

There's a secret entity called A-60 in the game's hidden area called The Rooms - a nod to an older Roblox horror game.

PRO SURVIVAL TIPS

LISTEN UP!

Sound is your biggest ally in this game. Entities like Rush and Ambush give away their presence before striking, so playing with headphones is recommended.

DON'T WASTE ITEMS

Save your vitamins for chases and only use your lighter or flashlight in dark rooms.

STAY WITH YOUR GROUP

If you're playing with friends, stick together. It's easier to survive when you're working as a team.

PEEK THROUGH DOORS

Sometimes you can see what's ahead before fully committing to the entrance. Use that split second to assess in order to avoid any surprises.

STICKY FINGERS

Check drawers and desks in early rooms to stock up. But don't get too greedy - Timothy the spider has a 1/200 chance of jumping out when you open a drawer.

THE FINAL CHALLENGE?

Once you reach Door 100, you'll face a tense puzzle-and-stealth finale. It's not just about hiding anymore - it's about solving under pressure. Can you stay calm and make it through?

Surviving DOORS isn't just about speed or skill - it's about paying attention, staying cool, and learning from every run. And when you do finally beat it? There's no better flex.

ALL STARS: BEDWARS

Some games are all about survival. Others are about building, battling, or strategy. Some games are about all of the above... and beds.

BedWars stands as a fan favorite in Roblox's combat scene, mixing strategic block-building with high-energy PvP and game modes that keep things fresh. With more beds than you'd find in a flagship IKEA, your mission is clear: protect your bed, destroy everyone else's.

It sounds simple. It is. But don't let that fool you. Winning a round of BedWars takes more than just swinging a sword. It takes planning, speed, creativity, and just the right amount of chaos.

ALL STARS PROFILE

NAME:	BedWars
PUBLISHER:	Easy.gg
GENRE:	Action
CREATED:	May 28th, 2021
VISITS:	10.4 billion +

BEDWARS

[BED BARRIER] BedWars
82% 16.1K
By [Content Deleted 5774246]
Updates are EVERY FRIDAY at 3:00pm PDT, 6:00pm EDT How to play Bed...

NEW TO BEDWARS?

It's best to start in Squads mode, where you can learn from your teammates. If you're brand new, check out the Training Area!

PICK YOUR PLAYGROUND

All game modes are accessible from the main lobby. Each one changes how the game feels, from fast solo fights to chaotic team battles.

GAME MODE	MODE FEATURES	NOTE
SOLO	1 player per team, 8 teams	You do everything yourself: defend, fight, and upgrade.
DOUBLES	2 players per team	Split responsibilities with your teammate.
SQUADS	4 players per team	Great for teamwork, longer matches, and big battles.
30 V 30	Total chaos	Huge maps, big resource fights, nonstop rushes.
LUCKY BLOCK	Classic rules, but with totally random items	Open lucky blocks to get anything from fireballs to throwable ducks.

PRO WARFARE TIPS

Want to actually win your matches, not just survive a few minutes? Let's break down the tactics top players use (and the mistakes you'll want to avoid).

EARLY GAME: FIRST 60 SECONDS

- Buy wool immediately and protect your bed, even if it's just a basic cover.
- Scout your neighbours. If they're already bridging, get ready to fight.
- Split tasks if you're playing in a team. Assign a defender, someone to gear up, and someone to rush mid/enemy beds.

MID GAME: CONTROL AND COMBAT

- Head to diamond generators to upgrade your team's armor, forge or trap.
- Rush mid for emeralds to use for upgrading your swords, pearls, or invis potions.
- Rotate between attack and defense, and don't tunnel vision on just one enemy.

LATE GAME: STAY SMART

- No bed = sudden death. Now you're out if you fall or get KO'd.
- Stack up gear like emerald armour, pearls, golden apples, and enchants.
- Stick with teammates; you're always safer in numbers.

PRO TIP:

If you're on your own, always check the kill feed and look around. Knowing who's eliminated or distracted gives you a huge edge.

TACTIC?

Grab diamonds and run. Don't try to fight over them early - secure your upgrades first, then go back for more.

PRO TIP:

In final 1v1s, build upward. Height gives you knockback advantage... Just don't fall.

ENTITY ESCAPE

The Entities of DOORS are creeping around every corner - can you make it through the maze without bumping into any of them?

Check out pages 62-63 for answers... if you dare.

BEDWARS BLOCK SEARCH

It's war! Can you find these BedWars Blocks in the wordsearch below?

If you need a hint, you can find the answers on pages 62-63!

Y	A	N	K	Y	L	O	S	A	U	R	U	S	D
K	A	P	P	A	K	I	D	U	E	C	O	K	I
D	K	O	A	V	P	A	R	A	K	E	E	T	O
D	R	C	N	E	G	L	E	E	E	L	S	U	O
F	L	E	B	A	H	I	V	A	D	E	N	O	U
E	Y	L	I	G	R	I	B	O	P	P	Y	K	E
E	N	O	O	N	L	W	P	B	J	H	A	C	S
S	X	T	A	R	D	O	H	L	O	A	J	E	R
H	Z	E	O	S	E	E	H	A	Y	N	E	G	O
U	L	C	E	Z	B	S	E	V	L	T	U	A	H
S	K	S	W	A	N	E	K	R	L	D	L	Y	R
K	K	N	U	M	P	I	H	C	K	E	B	B	E
Y	E	R	P	R	T	A	R	S	I	E	R	S	M
N	B	A	S	I	L	I	S	K	Y	Y	N	Z	A

WOOL
STONE
OBSIDIAN
TNT
DEFENDER
CAMERA
CLAY
GLASS
BRICK
LANTERN
LOG
LUCKY
RADIOACTIVE
CERAMIC

ALL STARS: NATURAL DISASTER SURVIVAL

ALL STARS PROFILE

NAME: Natural Disaster Survival
PUBLISHER: Stickmasterluke
GENRE: Survival
CREATED: March 29th, 2008
VISITS: 3.5 billion +

Surely this game requires no real introduction, but we'll go ahead and do it anyway for the sake of consistency. Natural Disaster Survival is one of the OG Roblox experiences, and it has managed to stick around since it first dropped all the way back in 2008, watching several of its old friends drop off into obscurity like they were catching strays from a meteor shower.

This round based adventure forces players to tap into their inner survival instincts. Each round kicks off with about 30-40 seconds to get yourself ready for whatever wild natural disaster is heading your way. Will it be rushing flash floods, shooting meteor showers or explosive volcanic eruptions? Oh, to name but a few.

Look out for the clouds having a white-lining during the 30-40 second prep period - that's a surefire sign a blizzard is on the way.

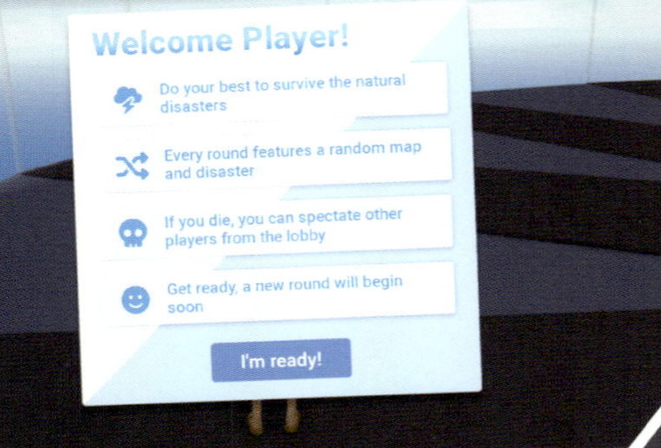

SURVIVAL GUIDE

There are thirteen different disasters in the game - some more fitting to the 'Natural' title than others (looking at you, acid rain) but all very much requiring tactics for survival. While every round is a breeding ground for chaos, here's a basic guide to making it through each disaster:

TORNADO

WEATHER: Cloudy
DURATION: 2 mins 10 secs

Tornados are super destructive, so make sure you stay far away from its path while still keeping an eye on it. Also be wary of flying debris; a piece could knock you straight off the island.

FLASH FLOOD

WEATHER: Cloudy
DURATION: 1 min 40 secs

This is one of the toughest disasters in the game to survive, so you have to spot it coming and prepare for a decent chance of survival. Try to locate the most stable looking structure to climb - NOT just the highest (that can result in you falling when it starts to crumble beneath you). If you do fall into the water, try to find a piece of floating debris to find refuge on.

Sometimes the game will throw the dreaded Multi-Disaster round at you, combining disasters for one big chaotic elemental hellscape for you to endure!

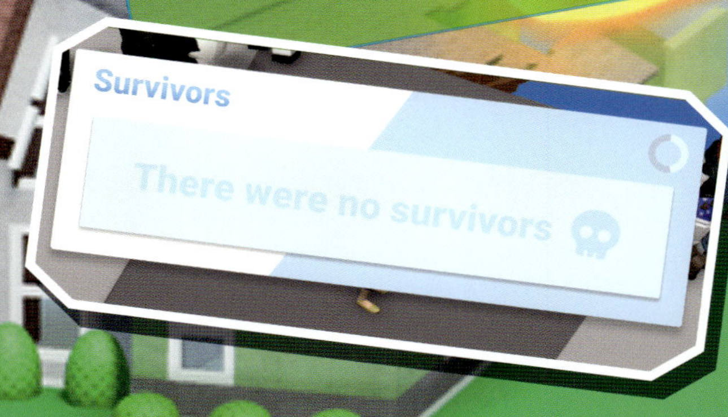

THUNDER STORM

WEATHER: Cloudy
DURATION: 2 min 15 secs

Stay indoors and avoid heights when you hear the huge crack of thunder that announces this disaster's arrival. Even indoors, you'll have to keep moving, as the lightning can destroy walls and ceilings.

METEOR SHOWER

WEATHER: Sunny
DURATION: 2 min 5 secs

There are no warning signs for a meteor shower - but maybe no warning sign is a warning sign? When you've clocked it's a meteor shower, keep your eye on the skies and be ready to dodge any incoming boulders. It's best to avoid being too high (too close to the meteor fall), and it's a good idea to keep moving around the edges of the island as they don't often strike there.

BLIZZARD

WEATHER: Cloudy/Snowy
DURATION: 2 min 10 secs

The snowstorm deals damage to anyone left out exposed, so seek shelter in the corner of a building to stay warm and wait it out.

FIRE

WEATHER: Sunny
DURATION: 2 min 15 secs

This is an easy disaster to survive as the fire moves pretty slowly. Just stick to the fringes of the map.

TSUNAMI

WEATHER: Sunny
DURATION: 2 min 10 secs

Thoughts and prayers, because a tsunami is serious business. Find high ground, but avoid tall and thin structures as they collapse easily.

SANDSTORM

WEATHER: Cloudy/Dusty
DURATION: 2 min 10 secs

The actual sandstorm won't deal any damage, but the flying bricks will certainly take you out if you get in their way. The best chance of survival is to actually stay outdoors and away from any buildings. Try to work out which direction the wind is blowing in and stand there for a safer wait (ex. If the bricks are flying to the North, stay on the South).

ACID RAIN

WEATHER: Cloudy
DURATION: 2 min 15 secs

Needless to say you're going to need to find shelter for this one, because this acid rain is corrosive. But it's not enough to just stay put and wait - keep an exit route in mind as the rain can burn through bricks, and you'll have to stay mobile to keep cover.

Listen out for the sound of the wind when the round starts. If you hear it howling, then that means Acid Rain is on its way.

EARTHQUAKE

WEATHER: Sunny
DURATION: 2 min 20 secs

The key to surviving an earthquake in-game isn't quite as obvious as some of the other disasters. The key is to keep jumping (on grass, preferably), as being mid-air keeps you unaffected by the shaking. You'll also need to keep an eye out for flying bricks trying to strike you off the island.

DEADLY VIRUS

WEATHER: Sunny
DURATION: 2 min 15 secs

This disaster is unique in that one player will be randomly selected as Patient Zero, and be infected by the virus. If you're lucky to escape that honoured role, then isolate yourself immediately and stay out of any grubby, germy clutches.

VOLCANIC ERUPTION

WEATHER: Sunny
DURATION: 2 min 25 secs

Exploding lava is predictably difficult to dodge, so all you can do is stay as far from the volcano as possible - this means the flaming lava bricks are less likely to hit you directly, and you'll be able to outmaneuver any that slowly roll your way. Stay alert and stay mobile to stay alive.

AVALANCHE

WEATHER: Sunny
DURATION: 2 min

To survive an avalanche, you need to find yourself a barrier from the oncoming snow. Sturdy structures will shield you, which is important, as even just touching the snow causes you damage.

DISASTER CROSSWORD

If there's one thing you've got to know to survive in Natural Disaster Survival, it's your natural disasters. Can you work out the clues and fill out the crossword below with the game's disasters?

Check out pages 62-63 for answers!

1 2 3 4 5 6 7 8 9 10

CLUES

ACROSS

2 Find cover! You don't want to get struck. (12)

3 Achoo! (6, 5)

4 Uh-oh, the ocean levels are rising! Find high ground! (5,5)

7 It's getting hot, hot, hot. (8, 8)

9 Brr... did anyone bring a scarf? (8)

10 This desert disaster is deadly and dusty. (9)

DOWN

1 This disaster comes from outer space. (6, 6)

5 Have you ever seen a wave that big? (7)

6 You can't even trust the ground you're standing on. (10)

8 Umbrellas aren't going to help you here. (4, 4)

SPOT THE DISASTER DIFFERENCE

Can you spot the differences between the two disasters? There are eight differences in total.

Check out pages 62-63 for answers!

HONOURABLE MENTIONS II

Still not convinced there are hidden treasures lurking in Roblox's endless catalog? Well, buckle up because we're diving even deeper into the vault of underrated awesomeness. These experiences might not have millions of players or flashy promotional campaigns, but they've got something even better: that special sauce that turns a random Tuesday night into an unforgettable gaming session.

Whether you're burned out on the usual suspects or just hunting for your next obsession, these picks are about to remind you why exploring Roblox feels like having access to an infinite arcade.

ROYALE HIGH

PUBLISHER: CALLMEHBOB

GENRE: ALL

This fantasy RPG masterpiece just got a major glow-up with stunning new visuals and an absolutely spellbinding story mode that'll have you completely mesmerized. We're talking about a world where you can live your best magical school life, attending classes by day and attending glamorous balls by night, all while rocking the most gorgeous outfits your Robux can buy. Whether you're mastering elemental powers, exploring enchanted realms, or just showing off your latest diamond-tier look, Royale High delivers that premium fairytale experience that makes every other game feel ordinary. If you've ever dreamed of being the main character in your own magical story, this is your moment to shine!

BLUE LOCK: RIVALS

PUBLISHER: BLUE LOCK RIVALS UNOFFICIAL FANS

GENRE: SPORTS & RACING

Think you've got what it takes to become the ultimate striker? Blue Lock: Rivals brings the ruthless, ego-driven world of the hit anime straight to your screen in the most intense football showdowns you've ever experienced. This isn't your typical friendly match; we're talking high-stakes 5v5 battles where only the strongest, most selfish players rise to the top. It's football, but with anime superpowers and enough competitive intensity to make your heart race.

MURDER MYSTERY 2

PUBLISHER: NIKILIS

GENRE: SURVIVAL

Murder Mystery 2 has mastered the art of turning friends into enemies faster than you can say "sus". Step into one of three thrilling roles: the sharp-eyed sheriff trying to solve the case, an innocent desperately trying to survive, or the sneaky murderer plotting everyone's demise. Your mission? Detect the killer, stay alive long enough to see justice served... or eliminate every last witness before your cover gets blown. It's social deduction gaming at its absolute peak, and honestly, the trust issues you'll develop are totally worth it.

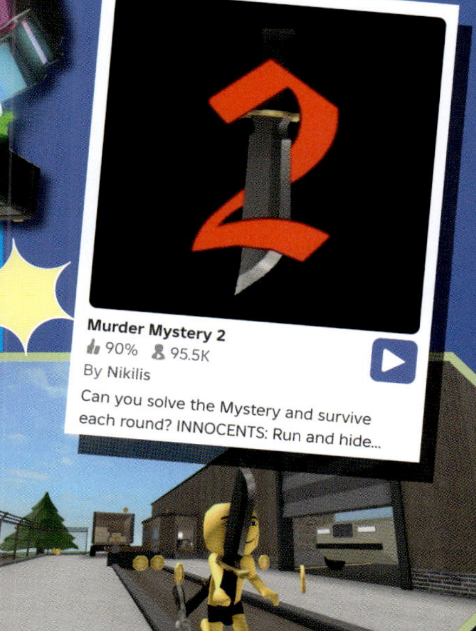

RESTAURANT TYCOON 2

PUBLISHER: ULTRAW

GENRE: SIMULATION

Ready to become the ultimate food empire mogul? Restaurant Tycoon 2 lets you build your culinary kingdom from the ground up, starting with nothing but big dreams and an empty lot. You're not just throwing together some random tables and calling it a day - you're the chef, interior designer, business strategist, and customer service guru all rolled into one ambitious little Gordon Ramsay-to-be. Warning: you might start furiously judging restaurants IRL after playing this.

PIGGY

PUBLISHER: MINITOON

GENRE: SURVIVAL

Okay, let's be real - if you don't know Piggy, you've been living under a Roblox rock. This survival horror masterpiece might not have snagged an All Stars spot this time around, but it's still absolutely legendary. Picture this: zombie apocalypse meets homicidal pig with a baseball bat. Your mission? Team up with fellow survivors, hunt down keys, and try to outsmart your bacon-colored nemesis without becoming pig food yourself. It's way more intense than your average hide-and-seek game, plus there's enough lore to keep conspiracy theorists busy for weeks. Trust us, once you start digging into the post-apocalyptic storyline, you'll be hooked harder than well... one of Piggy's victims.

WELCOME TO BLOXBURG

PUBLISHER: BLOXBURG DEVELOPMENT

GENRE: ROLEPLAY

Ever wanted to live the perfect suburban life without any of the real-world stress? Bloxburg is basically The Sims but way more social and infinitely more addictive! Build your dream house brick by brick, get a job to fund your fancy furniture addiction, and live out all your interior design fantasies. Whether you want to be a responsible adult with a proper career or just throw house parties 24/7, this life simulation lets you do it all. Fair warning: you may develop an obsession with kitchen layouts.

STEAL A BRAINROT

PUBLISHER: BRAZILIAN SPYDER

GENRE: SIMULATION

Get ready for the most ridiculously chaotic heist game you've ever played! The concept is beautifully simple: steal everyone else's Brainrot while desperately protecting your own from getting snatched. It's like a twisted game of keep-away where everyone's both the thief and the target. What's a Brainrot, you ask? Like... where do we even begin. Just boot it up to find out for yourself and you'll see why this game got 500 million visits in just one month after launch.

FORSAKEN

PUBLISHER: FORSAKEN DEV TEAM

GENRE: SURVIVAL

Think you can handle being trapped in your worst nightmare? Forsaken throws you into a terrifying game of cat and mouse where 10 players desperately try to survive while killers hunt them down one by one. Whether you're frantically completing objectives as a survivor or embracing your dark side as a killer, every match is pure adrenaline-pumping chaos. This asymmetric horror experience has taken Roblox by storm, and honestly, it's not hard to see why - nothing beats that heart-pounding moment when you realise the killer is right behind you!

ROBOT 64

PUBLISHER: ZKEVIN

GENRE: ADVENTURE

Meet Beebo, the most adorable robot with the most ridiculous mission ever: destroy the sun using ice cream! This delightfully bonkers 3D platformer draws serious inspiration from classic games like Super Mario 64, but cranks the weirdness up to eleven. You'll bounce, jump, and explore your way through the colorful world of Papatopia, collecting power-ups and mastering tricky platforming challenges. It's pure nostalgic platforming joy with a healthy dose of "wait, did I really just shoot ice cream at the sun?" energy that'll keep you grinning the entire time.

SORCERER'S AWAKENING

PUBLISHER: FARMERJALLER

GENRE: MEDIEVAL

What happens when you take Star Wars and drop it in the middle of a medieval fantasy world? Sorcerer's Awakening. Sure, the game might be pretty much retired at this point, but it's still worth checking out if you've ever wondered what lightsaber duels would look like with swords and sorcery. This medieval fantasy RPG takes everything you love about that galaxy far, far away and gives it a fantasy twist that feels both familiar and completely fresh.

INSIDE THE STUDIO

So you've played your way through all of the games we've recommended (and probably others you've spotted along the way) - but you still couldn't find something to scratch that very particular gaming itch you've been having? Well, why not try to make your own. Yeah, seriously.

No previous game development experience? No problemo. Roblox Studio is the ultimate creation toolkit, built so anyone (literally anyone) can jump in and build a game that's 100% their own.

ROBLOX Studio

Roblox Studio is available on both PC and Mac.

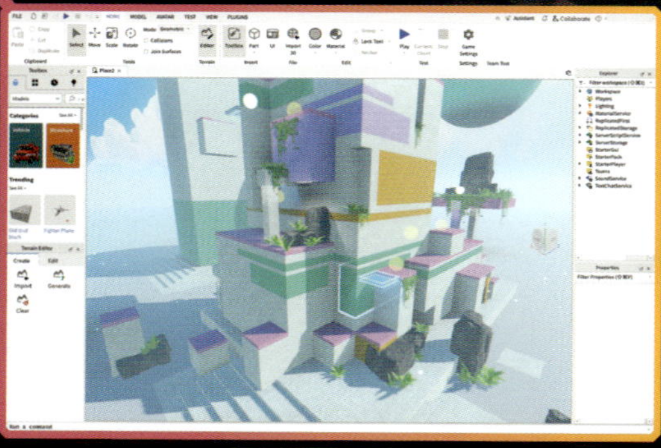

GETTING STARTED

When you fire up Roblox Studio, the screen should look something like the image above. From here, you've got access to a lineup of premade templates to kickstart your creation. If this is your first time diving in, we recommend starting with the Platformer template. It's a simple, no fuss game type that's perfect for learning the ropes.

Devs recommend a 2-button mouse with a scroll wheel for the easiest experience using Roblox Studio.

Make anything you can imagine

Everything you need to start creating on Roblox.
Join a thriving community of creators!

Start Creating

CREATING AND EDITING

Alright, so let's say you went with the Platformer template. Now you're staring at a new window that looks... a little overwhelming. Menus, buttons, dropdowns everywhere. But don't freak out - it's way easier to get the hang of than it looks.

The key thing to focus on? That big window in the middle. That's your game world. What you see there is what your players will see when they hit play. You can click, drag, and tweak parts of the environment right from this view. Want to move platforms around? Change colours? Add something new? This is where it all happens. Think of it as your virtual sandbox.

The beauty of using a template is that some of the heavy lifting is already done for you. Core mechanics (like where the game starts and ends) are baked in, along with a bunch of ready-made obstacles to get you going. From here, you've got total creative control. It's your world now - build it your way.

It might feel like a lot to digest at first, but don't worry - once you start playing around, it'll all begin to click. Spend some time exploring the menus, experimenting with the sliders, and just seeing what everything does. The more you dig in and mess around, the more confident you'll get, and the more creative control you'll have when building your own game from scratch.

PUBLISHING TO ROBLOX

Once you're done tinkering and happy with your creation, it's go-time! Just head to File > Publish to Roblox. You'll need to fill in a few quick details (like your game's name, a description, an icon, and the genre) and after that? You're live. You can jump in and play your own game, and even better - share it with the world so others can join the fun too.

FILE

		Recent Games
New	⌘N	1 My First Obby
Open from File...	⌘O	2 My First Obby
Open from Roblox...	⇧⌘O	
Close Place	⌘F4	
Save to File		
Save to File As...	⇧⌘S	
Save to Roblox		
Save to Roblox As...		
Publish to Roblox	⌥P	
Publish to Roblox As...	⌥⇧P	
Advanced	▸	
Game Settings...		
Studio Settings...	⌥S	
Beta Features		
Online Help...	F1	
About Roblox Studio		

Ready to level up your creations? If you really want to find out what Roblox Studio is capable of, check out the official guide at https://create.roblox.com/docs/tutorials

It's packed with everything you'll need to go from beginner to pro-builder, covering everything from the basics to more advanced stuff like coding and 3D modeling. If you're serious about creating something next-level, this guide is your go-to.

DID YOU KNOW?

Roblox is full of secrets, surprises, and seriously awesome stats - and we've packed this page with the coolest ones! From jaw-dropping player numbers to wacky in-game wonders, these facts will blow your avatar's Limited U socks off. We bet there's something here you didn't know.

THE NATION OF ROBLOX

Over 70 million people play Roblox every single day. That's more than the population of the United Kingdom! If Roblox were a country, it would be one of the top 20 most populated places on Earth.

MY, HOW YOU'VE GROWN

Roblox has grown by over 100,000% in daily active players since 2010. Back then, only about 20,000 people logged in daily. Now it's over 70 million - that's like every single person in France jumping online at once!

SHE'S GLOBAL

From the USA to Zimbabwe, Roblox has players on nearly every continent (sorry, Antarctica penguins). That's officially more international than the Olympics!

PROJECT ZERO

The first Roblox game was made way back in 2006! That means Roblox has been around since flip phones were in, YouTube was brand new, and dinosaurs (and by dinosaurs, we mean elderly millennials) still roamed MySpace.

40 MILLION+

There are more than 40 million experiences on Roblox. If you played a new one every hour, nonstop, it would take you over 4,500 years to play them all. So good luck with that.

PERSONAL STYLE

There are billions of avatar outfits on Roblox. In fact, over 165 million items were created by users in just one year! From sparkly wings to pizza hats, there's something to suit everyone's tastes (lack of judgement not guaranteed, though).

YOU'RE A WIZARD

Roblox had over 1.1 trillion hours of playtime in 2023. That's enough time to watch the entire Harry Potter series more than 300 billion times, or a casual walk to the moon and back 1 million times over.

PET POPULARITY

The most popular experience on the platform is undoubtedly Adopt Me! It once had over 1.9 million players online at the same time. That's like filling up 30 football stadiums with Roblox fans.

EVERY DAY IS A NEW DAY

More than 100,000 new experiences are published daily. Let that number sink in for a moment next time you complain about having nothing to play.

SCREEN STAR

80% of Roblox playtime happens on the mobile, but you can also play Roblox on PC, Mac, Xbox, and even some VR headsets. Basically, if it has a screen, it's probably ready for Roblox.

ANSWERS

16 ADOPT ME! RARE PET SEARCH

Y	A	N	K	Y	L	O	S	A	U	R	U	S	D
K	A	P	P	A	K	I	D	U	E	C	O	K	I
D	K	O	A	V	P	A	R	A	K	E	E	T	O
D	R	C	N	E	G	L	E	E	E	L	S	U	O
F	L	E	B	A	H	I	V	A	D	E	N	O	U
E	Y	L	I	G	R	I	B	O	P	P	Y	K	E
E	N	O	O	N	L	W	P	B	J	H	A	C	S
S	X	T	A	R	D	O	H	L	O	A	J	E	R
H	Z	E	O	S	E	E	H	A	Y	N	E	G	O
U	L	C	E	Z	B	S	E	V	L	T	U	A	H
S	K	S	W	A	N	E	K	R	L	D	L	Y	R
K	K	N	U	M	P	I	H	C	K	E	B	B	E
Y	E	R	P	R	T	A	R	S	I	E	R	S	M
N	B	A	S	I	L	I	S	K	Y	Y	N	Z	A

17 GUESS THE PET

1. Happy Duckling
2. Dragon
3. Kitsune
4. Yeti
5. Unicorn
6. Penguin
7. Bird of Paradise
8. Tiger

20 SPRING GARDENING

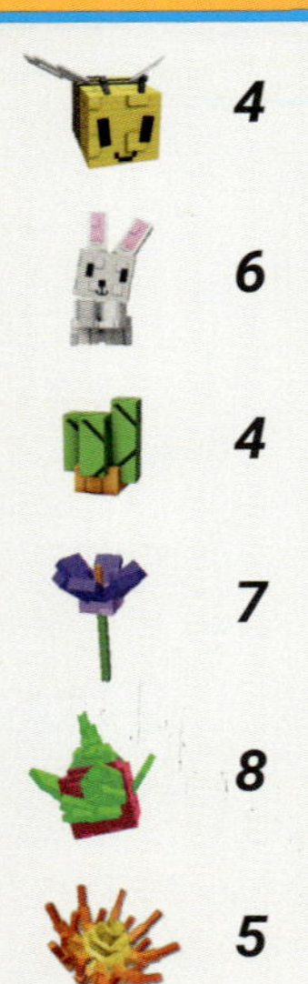

4

6

4

7

8

5

3

6

8

3

7

9

21 GARDEN MAZE

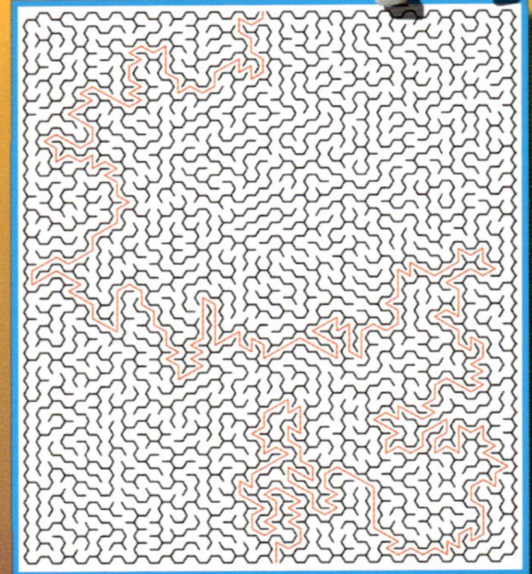

24 MAZE OF HELL

25 SPOT THE DIFFERENCE